CW00432979

THIS NOTEBOOK BELONGS TO:

____

ISBN: 9798643405832